INTERLOCUTOR GODDESS

INTERLOCUTOR GODDESS

JASMINE REID

WINNER OF THE 2024 CAAPP BOOK PRIZE

Interlocutor Goddess

Published by Autumn House Press

ISBN: 978-1-63768-111-4

Cover Art: Mel Walton
Book and Interior Design: Melissa Dias-Mandoly
Author Photo: Nico Reano

Library of Congress Cataloging-in-Publication Data

Names: Reid, Jasmine (Poet) author
Title: Interlocutor goddess / Jasmine Reid.
Description: Pittsburgh : Autumn House Press, 2025.
Identifiers: LCCN 2025015555 (print) | LCCN 2025015556 (ebook) | ISBN 9781637681114 paperback | ISBN 9781637681121 epub
Subjects: LCGFT: Poetry
Classification: LCC PS3618.E5348 I58 2025 (print) | LCC PS3618.E5348 (ebook) | DDC 811/.6--dc23/eng/20250520
LC record available at https://lccn.loc.gov/2025015555
LC ebook record available at https://lccn.loc.gov/2025015556

Printed in the United States on acid-free paper that meets the international standards of permanent books intended for purchase by libraries.

Autumn House Press is a nonprofit corporation whose mission is the publication and promotion of poetry and other fine literature. The press gratefully acknowledges support from individual donors, public and private foundations, and government agencies.

This book was supported, in part, by The Pittsburgh Foundation, the Greater Pittsburgh Arts Council, and the Pennsylvania Council on the Arts, a state agency funded by the Commonwealth of Pennsylvania.

This book was published in partnership with the Center for African American Poetry and Poetics.

for little jasmine, with unconditional love

TABLE OF CONTENTS

Nebula Elsewhere

escape velocity 7

Nebula Elsewhere 8

Goddess writes 13

the poet of flowers

looking up, the poet of flowers writes:
nothing holds the stars 17

crush 18

nectarean hymen 19

a bed of beauty until alive, bury me 20

swing s(onn)et 21

waterful jasmine 22

swing s(onn)et 23

this i rotary 24

conjoined terror-reel & still-life 29

Bloom Psychotherapy

chromosome death in a blood garden 33

~~daughter~~ ~~(daughter)~~ ~~*daughter*~~ **daughter** 34

a kind of death flower 36

The Moon and the You Tree 37

a stroke / of dirt 38

toy chest 43

parent rock 44

not a suicide note 45

terminal threshold 46

ars poetica 47

the nest of nothing

the nest of nothing 51

The Angel Of Blank

epi-visage from The Angel Of Blank 77

suppliant women 79

building the barricade 80

dead, doing, dying, live 81

dis · cover 82

subjectivity 83

mars poetica 85

(puberty too)

redwood forest 89

at twenty-six, hugs are dangerous 90

state wax, state wane 91

color is a transitionary state of emergency 92

please in ultramarine 93

she harvests herself 94

puberty 2 95

self-sentence 96

Certificate of Live Birth 97

CERTIFICATION OF VITAL RECORD 98

VITAL 99

of devotion, angel 100

Goddess

interlocutor litany 104

girl is only everywhere 105

where all, we flowers 106

trans: atlantic 107

Apocrypha: i exist in every world 108

perigee 109

concatenate theory: a cosmology: a hole 110

i did not become, but i was, i am, i will be, born 111

dearly beloved 112

Traverse Town 113
she 114
stars poetica 115

Notes 117
Acknowledgments 119

INTERLOCUTOR GODDESS

"Let the world eat me, but
then, let the world sob, not me."

—Sandra Lim

"Must answer to time.
Time dictates all else, except some. It misses."

—Theresa Hak Kyung Cha

"and she was tra
velling across that middle pass
age, constantly coming from wh
ere she had come from—in her"

—Kamau Brathwaite

Nebula Elsewhere
the poet of flowers
Bloom Psychotherapy
the nest of nothing
The Angel Of Blank
(puberty too)
Goddess

escape velocity

porch steps   swing set
            batty bwhy   i was small
            small why   small sad   not allowed
loud   now   heave   heave

rumble
shed

            reach
            shed
                              retch
                              shed

good   bye   heart   bye   closer   closer
                                                                        her

Nebula Elsewhere

aster risked at birth
freak   freak
playground in the mind
little flowergirl
swing   set   dusk
me
me
me
.

doctor says
where does it hurt?
draw   my   blood
here
here:

[ ]?

black blank at the brink of bell
swing at which i shell
last earth record of self
swell, swell   back to gyell
when every blood-body said freak   &   hell
you swung off to somewhere else
ring?   ring?   flower-knell
look!   girl   spring
well

unto the nowhere that holds the stars & everything

else. hurtling to nevermore & ever-else

i try to see the hyper-hued faces of now

but the future tense is where i'll bleak & all

the monuments of here go bust along the way

& i am so, so sorry   i am the blank

i am the bleep   i am, forever

rip in the sky   rip in the family-earth

heave hurt
weave her

(two pink pills , three blue pills)

Jasmine? Jasmine?

.

light

light

light

i whorl world
girl go go
starburst
weave thread thicker than family
line line line

i

was knot
tug   loop
follow through over through over
the moon construct
to aqueduct dust
to ring light   my dark face

constantlycomingwater
\
·   —   fromwhereshewater
/
hadcomefromwater

my dark face
moon eye over tide
to slosh or drip   to be hold

i   go   go   go

engine: estrogen

supernova hypertrophied girlgender
ring, my neck   thirteen planets of girl
Me in the face   (world)
Me in the face   (world)

❀

let there be *ma'am* in my direction

light is not the river of my reflection

please don't he   be leaf   she-stream

unstoppered green

flowers girl   in swing sets   play ground in a grove of galaxy

little jasmine in space   another name for gravity

Goddess writes

poet, gesture me to your blood work, pro pulse!
will you hold your ear to our congenital wound?
resonate your holes with my holes.
hear the bigness of space our cosmological ow, surrownd.

how different our lives would be, dear flower, if never was the word
"freak" placed on me & where, in place,
i was always named "fecundity"

resuscitate

pressed into the nothing-nest. ear the sibilances

~~belong~~ be loam!
uncongeal the blood-lawed garden

to otherwise illuminate wounded aureoles, to lighten fallen orioles,
collect their small gasps, mother coos

fecund, fecund, fecund, fecund, fecund, fecund, fecund

Nebula Elsewhere
the poet of flowers
Bloom Psychotherapy
the nest of nothing
The Angel Of Blank
(puberty too)
Goddesss

looking up, the poet of flowers writes: ***nothing holds the stars***

then, sweet
Pisces,

squeeze my aster-hand,
push the riskéd meet.

pull the sorry dandelion out of me,
then suck your teeth.

blow me a way,
puddle-bud or pirouetting pollen.

see, you make do
& i do. i do.

crush

your hand swells my neck, *pretty*, you say
i am, no matter how decimal-small.
my eyelash flutters across your shoulder.
gravity. you land on my chest skin—
breast swelled *pretty*—shut my jaw
hmmm. atmos-. lips.
pink wisps. my nimbus'd *yes*
says, *make me blue in the face as the day i was born.*
years crushed into nothing between us

bright & assigned as birth. girl. garments.
collide me all over under your thumb.
pink pants. i am learning breath.
reviving choke. not between,
but down my legs you go,
saying how long they are, saying, *your eyebrows are fucking perfect.*

my best parts: between your teeth.
at most fear, i furthest live.
squeeze.
i'd give my meteor-
ological plead, my knees.
anything to be the pretty
girl inside your hands.
your hands inside your girl.

nectarean hymen

maple lip gloss   sticky skin   everybody look fly-ugly
stuck   today-hah hid my hide
hyme so sticky & pretty   sky
hi am princess please   royal blue gravity. (   ) grasp
my nips crowned stiff in the night's grass mouth   hi miss
bare me but b-words   bears bees
sun-suck-curse-all so honey moon concealer outside
rouge not rue-in   hah
inside leaves shake like leaves in sight   in stead
of "run" high flower hand hope for thorns
trees to look up to   under this season
of fear   oh Autumn
where did all my person go

a bed of beauty until alive, bury me

say i was a careless shutting
of language an accident
sound whirling into the guttur

grimacing certificates of sir
survive shoreline immeasurable
find me in rivulets

jostled at the sight of stars
tonight i saw salted over
the small town of my yearning i

showed my face to all their light
& did not feel ugly
meeting alive i say

because the sight of my insides is out & sound
oh Goddess i am finally sheen

swing s(onn)et

July memories my very first kissed . . .
falling its pieces leaves you lets you withhold
the ground *swaan maan* this asterisk it's not fair
your name sounds distress my o's rag into
we table the taller hopes in me beneath the carve
swoon moon skirt i pleat at wilt-me eyes let-me rope
around your mounding yes almond-pleased
golden *brawn* you roll my bones out of joint
the upright willow weeps *brown* leagues of summer rain
tomorrow's mud is now our watered way
tight touch falls *down* the plateau grass
the hills tip our heads tap hashed out aureole *dawn*
titillative taste of pink skin strawberries tumble
listing under jazz clouds we up on toes tilt

waterful jasmine

bud is the skin my rouge
swell of flower / flesh
busy with becoming rayed
her hand on my cheek
is a touch of water to leaf
announcing, pulling, slowly
the sky / river of her face & me
open lips part the atmosphere of far / away
& she says, *lovely*, i am
beautiful, i am
in her mouth-touch, i am
resuscitated light :/: the ash of our sound
sweet   open   caramelized moan
my flowermouth

nascent & petal-nothing
i go the way of an infant / star

swing s(onn)et

listing under jazz clouds we up on toes tilt
titillative taste of pink skin strawberries tumble
the hills tip our heads tap hashed out aureole *dawn*
tight touch falls *down* the plateau grass
tomorrow's mud is now our watered way
the upright willow weeps *brown* leagues of summer rain
golden *brawn* you roll my bones out of joint
around your mounding yes almond-pleased
swoon moon skirt i pleat at wilt-me eyes let-me rope
we table the taller hopes in me beneath the carve
your name sounds distress my o's rag into
the ground *swaan maan* this asterisk it's not fair
falling its pieces leaves you lets you withhold
July memories my very first kissed . . .

this i rotary

ablution in the scoundrel field
my little sincere lungs
out a meridian longing as skein
a red-lacquered sky salutation
acorns ladled in Autumn tumble
over head & parishioner grass
poor nut cases lose their hats
stiff & scattered seeds beside the nutter tree
a glib hello

infertile flower
balled up fisted pulp dribbled
unto the morrow i live more mesome
titrate true each flying forage—spill
over her under her upside downside gluttonous
glamorous glimmer dipper
stacks & stacks of me

little school of light & sound,
throttle into awe. telescope.
moon copse. babbling look. i am part & port.
imported part. imparted port. concrete
crushed into stars. devotion.

cull cord languish   cut   string   spring
hickory-call lickety whirl
mouth monthing sherwood
cream cumberland   Daisy's la

Somesday Starsday Wondersday
Watersday Windsday Livesday Liveday

conjoined terror-reel & still-life

pretty in deracinated repose
roots over mattress reach—
slate sheets pool on the kitchen floor—abscess lux
roots under slats & calyx bitter-black
birds go on singing despite veil & shrugging sky shoulder slopes
how shriveling, lingua metastatic spittle
tongue eaten by a new corona—dream
in waveform violet, tongued & cumming true
snow green in a forest of doors
sprouting leaves repotted in *please*
when will my labial fold
split me chasm-reel & tulip-life
still as entrance, still as exit
discharging so much gray
please, May, make a vagina out of me
take my glans, push the meet

Nebula Elsewhere

    the poet of flowers

        Bloom Psychotherapy

            the nest of nothing

        The Angel Of Blank

    (puberty too)

Goddess

chromosome death in a blood garden

call grass the clutch so here we are
before agony in the garden
mom ripped to   what hands hold
tinker-fertile remaining   blood let to blood left
under earth   daughter shed   shears pliers
(fecund fecund)
something luciferous in the sentence
ex-spelled under sunday school
danced on devil pediphilia stomped pediphobia stamped
pisspot shitbox wormed decomposite expresses
nonetheless x   mark end   mark begin
gather treeward   root of root   recompose   little y
vined other side
not heaven but riven

daughter (daughter) *daughter* daughter

forgive the first thing about me
detachment a cavity called chest
before milk there was gravity
the small thud of singular blood
drown is out the self-sounds a heart makes
flooding herself with herself
medicalized murmur wis—purr-pitch
nub of nothing pinched
boy oh boy you a-chorusing still

forget the first thing about me
i am not the shell of you divided by his seed
if i was born anything it is distance
immeasurable in the plane of looking
i am expelled at first glance struck
where you were cut there is a nurse
overseeing epidural my one heart
arrested by fault already dead inside you
buzz buck pulse shock of emerging see
section every day this dying too
un-name your wound when will you
hear me out i was not born
unto kingdom but sliced from fluid forgiveness
embryonic years & years my knees flung wide
for the world's concision
holly bells of you ringing under my skin

away from you i stand orthoscopic
in a full-grown body under amniotic waters
stilling me my name the many days
i have peeled & purpled climbed the vines
spreading like a rumor all along
a tower fleshed moment splitting vision
your many voices arriving sirens
find me falsely accuse of exiting
wrongly your womb a king above
the inverted cunt you call me
cuts sonographically through
the zero matter of what i choose
nothing : never : fists pounding my belly
night : terror : mother
i am trying so very hard not to hate you

a kind of death flower

bean sprout splitting spilling
seedless nothing no necro matter
alma mater unmother muttering
its meat unshuttering how it is vacant
see green shooting its mouth
peal after ceasing peal hallow wheel
squealing its lonely pittance softly
breaking ungrowing sheaf
to sheets radial downpour
millimeters vanishing underground
unquite a surface or sea

The Moon and the You Tree

Silly me, I raise tide eyes-high and diaphragm flips, hits
heart's Atlantic floor. Moon white cast on sand dial silt
and the sedge. Crescent gibbous squint as ships wreck
thump, thump, wood on shore, groaning.
Can't inlet or oar to soil. Motherland gone. A father's thick roots
buried in a distant city. And the you tree, worn, perennial, and far,
here as the unconsoling sky.

The Moon is my sister. All her light is second-handed.
A letting scar, a cooing wound. My feet are ballrooms
filled with gospel, my many organs conspiring to live.
The you tree's needle leaves feather my slip. I fall bluish rouged
bloodshot and bespectacled as two moons looking, looking.
Moon, can you see? We are black and alone.
Hobbled homonym of parting: part company, part cutlery.

Another gone knives into me. Moon can't sea,
her maria art dry bowls for faraway spoons.
Can't water without we. The you tree stirs stars above me.
I play the lark of darling in cold light. My corona borrowed
and pitiful. Nerves pace their halls, house of a dying child
I don't see. Every feeling crowded with hope.
There is only leaving and leaves

jabbing my back, drawing red longing onto grass.
Even bleeding crowded with hope. I reach for a sound
or a branch of touch. Its grasp after the stars,
the you tree says nothing, not a limb in reach.
Moon is full and red as Mars. A scar let loose.
Planetary as a heart. There is a hole between moon
and moan. I live here, in the silence, infant beneath the you tree,
    a devastated maroon.

a stroke / of dirt

when dad passed
a butterfly clapped
its wings & that's
the sound dearest
to silence a soul nearness
leaving prepared me nest
of nothing i am next
to nothing

mom said, at his funeral
i cried & asked, *where's dad? where's dad?*
i remember nothing of those months
only, after, the fleshy feeling of a hole
when thinking of him, an ache stemmed
my chin to chest, i fell into myself
thought i must be something
wrong to be so alone

i dug backyard, aged into the soil
horizon by horizon, expecting parent rock. i
pulled out a whole girl.
a hole & then, myself.
& so it was, my mother said,
if your father were still alive
he would have a fit. you know that,
don't you? he would have a fit.

spared him, i am she who stalks
tall as grass beneath the branch-working
swallow. i was born out of tongue
& only the dirt would have me.
i am a loam. i am alone. i am the lunacy
of living furled below loess, sediment, error.
anti-sentiment, here is wind. live. have your fit.
blood clot. kill me.

near-dead,
i am a facety face'd
hole-hearted
deciduous blank

toy chest

dad lacquered   rosewood toy chest
heart carved seat back
heart carved with what comes next

dad hole   toy chest

heart hole   my hand traces the would
i am told, in dad's other home
there is a room full of toys
i imagine stacks & stacks.
it is my favorite place.
when i am good, dad comes back with a toy,
a taste of the room i could swim through.
a wizard or a god, he rains good spells down on me;
beats me when i am bad, *Renez, pull the car over.*
i am torn , a-storm , a welted weather kicking in the backseat.
i am a kid & no one listens to me;
no one tells me where my father has gone.
i sit at the toy chest & feel; v hole . m hole
he mumbles in the dark. my father is a wizard;
he stumbles through the house. boom. boom.
i fall into my hole whenever i'm alone:
i go boooooooom. i go boooooooom. *boombie* he calls me,
cooks a second dinner after my bedtime
when i toddle into ma & dad's bedroom & say, *i'm hungry.*
that is the only parent sentence i know.

parent rock

when am i?

ribs-cave deposits from

tall? not tall?

sternum-body force

i miss my dad. i miss my dad.

schisty cleavage

there is a physic

a mass over memory

ghosts press on me

tear-thysts

my body presses on

grass above the bitterness

sudden apertures

i am not the 'ites i carry

projections laser off the cut

don't tell me i'm unhealable

look inside, *i am a holme*

not a suicide note

i have hidden the knives & safety razors
inside a bag inside a box inside a bag
under my bed
enclosures bare at the bark of my blood
disclosures keep these gallons in case
the tree-clovers have not yet called I
am urgency   the measure of my hands
from a blade   my feet from the lake
my brains from the bathroom sink
listen
i will not list my passwords & apologies
i will not tell you to bury me where the dirt can eat me
nor to shoot me into the nearest stellar nursery
i will not tell you of the gutter rat my mother has called me
nor the porcelain where my father's hands have sent her front teeth

i am not from here, after all, & was born like
infants unsuccessfully murdered into
the wrong in this world & learned the salvation of dirt
& sewers, something like resuscitation
to have been sent here
i must be the angel of something
shoving away blades & giving them skins
to live beneath my dreams
i must be the angel of something
sing, sing the stars & warm dark in my knees
infant Goddess, little universe sum
where blooms the common factor of my breaths
jasmines grow in threes
(i amb* i amb* i amb*)

terminal threshold

i want the day a road, river,
sentence crossed & carried as dust, muck,
period per-missing parent but   capital
punishment in Mourning there is
a genitive   ax cleaving each fresh
horizon, there is a silence—some clouds
put last lights to death—

there is an end to disbelief
if nothing else, the wind passes through me

a woman stares at my face until her stop
on the train
a man becomes a crane
his neck bends & bends until i look
up & he is a man again
white underneath pinkish blemishes
camelia flowers & squat horticultural shrubs
porch swing   & black-eyed Susans
a sun dressed in smoke & shadow
reaches my surface   i am not
as dervish as i appear   whirling
under a city'd tree
    older than all the mothers
& fathers in the world
i could grow beyond

ars poetica

the poems are branches worked through the mouth & hands.
a nest, a nest! a limbwork i can lie down in,
get up from

Nebula Elsewhere
the poet of flowers
Bloom Psychotherapy
the nest of nothing
The Angel Of Blank
(puberty too)
Goddess

the nest of nothing

Light is history in flames . . .
We need to know about the darkness where
dreams go and where we are

—June Jordan, "*On the Twenty-fifth Anniversary of the United Nations: 1970,*" *Directed by Desire*

in her talk, "The Family: Our Beloved Crisis," Hortense J. Spillers elucidates the family's character as an "organization of emotional resources" and as a concatenation of its history, its persons. historically, the family is an institution replicative of the social architectures of oppression, violence by force & omission, what Spillers calls "the social calculus of social demography."[1] the question, the crisis, she then follows: is freedom by definition a transcendence of family? family, the organization-organism designed to lock us down to certain roles & profit motives, racist & nationalist ideologies, how family embodies the capitalist state's secrets & inhibitions: "in place of ethical conduct," filial obligations & pieties of the blood form genderful obediences.[2] discipline imperative as a swing of the belt, the switch, the hand, a hush, a shush, a shut-up-the-noise-that-is-your-self. yet, by the circumstances of birth & state, family is, broadly, the de facto starting place, the nest into which human being after human being emerges. a hole, a stricture, a person-sized wound.

---

1 Spillers, Hortense J. "The Family: Our Beloved Crisis." 2019 M.H. Abrams lecture, 21 Mar 2019, Cornell University. *YouTube: Cornell English Department.*

2 ibid.

a nest: a structure or place made or chosen by a bird for laying eggs and sheltering its young.

a nest: a place filled with or frequented by undesirable people or things.[3]

as we consider emergence, starting place, & replication, return, dear reader, let us turn to Sigmund Freud's concept of the death drive, a principle which states that "the aim of all life is death," so articulated in *Beyond the Pleasure Principle*:

> Let us suppose, then, that all the organic instincts are conservative, are acquired historically and tend towards the restoration of an earlier state of things . . . Those instincts are therefore bound to give a deceptive appearance of being forces tending towards change and progress, whilst in fact they are merely seeking to reach an ancient goal by paths alike old and new.[4]

throughout *Beyond the Pleasure Principle,* Freud's thinking is a combinate of the scientific & the speculative. the scientific: evolution and intergenerational patterns, self-preservative instincts, lineage, how organisms re-create the forms that make them possible, how a nest is a concatenate theory: a cosmology: a hole. the speculative: a hypothesis of the origins of the cell as the fundamental structure of life ever-seeking through its processes of development (life) a return (death) to

---

3 *Oxford English Dictionary*, "Nest," accessed 16 Dec. 2019.

4 Freud, Sigmund. *Beyond the Pleasure Principle*, Trans. James Strachey. New York, New York: W.W. Norton & Company, Inc., 1961. 31-32. Print.

where life emerges, a life living to die to live, & the "opinion of many biologists that what [migratory birds of passage] are doing is merely to seek out the localities in which their species formerly resided but which in the course of time they have exchanged for others."[5] from nest to further nest to former nest. from be to undying be.

repeated across generations, these death-driven life instincts confound the linear model of our earthling experience of time, progression. rather, we move forward in order to return to earlier times, states, & occurrences. in this way, the shape of our lives is a recapitulation of the conditions of our birth, a shape that ends where it begins: the womb, nest, life-potentiality-space wherein we do not exist, yet, might.

how might we read a womb with & against the death drive as an attempt to close this loop, to return to life by giving life, to heal itself closed through the again & again of birth. is radical future-making possible within this mode of repetition, of return, these conservative instincts that Freud so names?

bound as death & life so are, in any order: the aim of all death is life.
a hole: world.
if my life is an attempt to heal my mother womb, wound, let us, then,

---

[5] ibid.

consider something of the essence of transness, the origin wound, the mis-assignation at birth (wound) simultaneous to the exiting (wound) of mother womb. must there, too, be a simultaneity of healing?

too, there is the *transition*, which gives the deceptive appearance of a shift forward in time, a progression away from mis-assignation to self-articulation, confounds in its secreted nature: to transition is to reach back to the primal pool of our potential, the womb in which things could have been different, from which we might have been correctly assigned or unassigned in the first place (nest) so that we can be the everything that we are (next). transness is a return, yes, a reconstruction, a ritual-repetition forward-backward to regain the potentiality of an earlier state. in this confluence fluidity of time (womb), there is the all we are and the all we will ever be.

in Freud's paper "Neurosis and Psychosis," he writes:

> The etiology common to the onset of a psychoneurosis and of a psychosis always remains the same. It consists of a frustration, a non-fulfillment, of one of those childhood wishes which are for ever undefeated and which are so deeply rooted in our phylogenetically determined organization.[6]

---

[6] Freud, Sigmund. "Neurosis and Psychoses." *The Standard Edition of the Complete Psychological Works of Sigmund Freud, Volume XIX (1923 - 1925): The Ego and the Id and Other Works*. Edited and translated by James Strachey. London: Hogarth Press, 1961. 151. Print.

oh, organization of frustration. while it is not my aspiration within this project to claim my transness as a psychosis, psychosis is nonetheless projected onto the transness within which i am rescued, nested, & the above remains salient to this work of peering over at the nest of place made or chosen for laying eggs, sheltering young, and repeating history. & so, dear reader, let us attune our attention to psychosis which, as it appears in the above, denotes a delusion, the manifestation of an attempt to resolve a conflict between the ego and the external world, a non-fulfillment of a wish, resulting in a separation from the external world. psychosis is a label affixed to those who disavow reality & are disavowed by reality. there is a physic at work here, this power of naming. to be trans, to be named delusional is to emerge from a severance from a narrow reality in which trans persons are not allowed to exist in the first place. nothing that i am, must i reckon with where i cease to exist completely, without remainder? in collaboration with how Theresa Hak Kyung Cha writes of "time" in her book *Dictee*, i will write of "family":

> must answer to *family*.
>
> *family* dictates all else, except some. it misses.[7]

---

[7] the original lines read: "Must answer to time. Time dictates all else, except some. It misses." Hak Kyung Cha, Theresa. *Dictee*. Berkeley: University of California Press, 2001. 40 - 41. Print.

in *Notes on the Phantom: A Complement to Freud's Metapsychology*, Nicolas Abraham writes, "It is the children's or descendants' lot to objectify these buried tombs through diverse species of ghosts. What comes back to haunt are the tombs of others."[8]

family (trauma) creates crypts, burial sites in our psyches, our repository of secrets. what is it to be haunted by the tombs of others? an unconsciousness which organizes, ventriloquizes the living. secreted in me, how *to secret* & *to secrete* become indistinguishable in the past tense. how to compose a story of these objects? being so far away . . . what happens when the circumstances of one's birth marks a separation from family? to be marked as deformed by family, unacceptable as queer, as trans, that i am, such that i am behind my starting place, my familial nest. the beyond of being behind . . . what can be found there, made there, lived there? this nest of nothing.

> when dad passed
> a butterfly clapped
> its wings & that's
> the sound dearest
> to silence a soul nearness

---

[8] Abraham, Nicolas. "Notes on the Phantom: A Complement to Freud's Metapsychology." *Critical Inquiry* 13.2, The Trial(s) of Psychoanalyses: (1987): 208. *JSTOR.* Feb 2019.

leaving prepared me nest
of nothing i am next
to nothing

if transness marks such a severe deviation from the familial organization-organism, nest-to-nest concatenation, that it is, in fact, a separation, a break from the indoctrination of family, history, & identity as national-political piety, then, too, there is within transness the radical potential of a freedom which makes for new possibilities of being, organizing, organism, world, reconfiguring what it means to be in a body & what a body might look like. from the spectral origin of nothing, we are alive, trained in the anti-past practice articulated by sociologist Avery Gordon in *Ghostly Matters: Haunting and the Sociological Imagination*:

> Following the ghost is about making a contact that changes you and refashions the social relations in which you are located . . . It is sometimes about writing ghost stories, stories that not only repair representational mistakes, but also strive to understand the conditions under which a memory was produced in the first place, toward a countermemory, for the future.[9]

[9] Gordon, Avery F. *Ghostly Matters: Haunting and the Sociological Imagination*. Minneapolis: University of Minnesota Press, 2008. 22. *ProQuest Ebook Central*. Web. Accessed Oct 2019. (I was first introduced through this text by Muriel Leung's poetic essay "This Is to Live Several Lives.")

in the nothing within which we are nest, there is contact with what might have been different, a something which haunts the absence of something, a ghostly togetherness. to exceed the family, too, to transcend it, in nothing, in transness, there is the potential "of an alternate diagnostics [whose purpose] is to link the politics of accounting, in all its intricate political-economic, institutional, and affective dimensions, to a potent imagination of what has been done and what is to be done otherwise."[10] to be outside the nest of undesirable somethings is to understand that the conditions which produce them are neither ever-present nor everlasting, is to return to what might have been different & recover oneself as a countermemory in order to project forward the sum things, what can be different.

black blank at the brink of bell
swing at which i shell
last earth record of self

i am a follow the shell i follow the shed i follow
the embellied feeling the infant swing the ring
the she the she the she the sexton that i am

in dirt-time the skeletal i ear
these spectral years to the day

---

10 ibid, 18.

my littlest flesh-&-born i hear
with the passing of years
these stethoscopic feels

in her collection, *feeld,* poet Jos Charles writes that a "feeld" can be understood as a "felt past thru."[11] a "lot" might be a feeld of past tombs present wounds

i taste the tunnel which pulsed
me through an infant-sized who
this loop   hole

in a blood garden, on a wire wrung day
i thought i would row out until my chromosome death,
these helical maps of me, too tired to swim back to see

the lot might be skin descended onto me. emergent blood i bloom my
surface into a garden replete with a diverse species of flower & star
shapes, dandelion seeds: my follicular

tok tok conversion of breath
little blood rudder i whoop
as it future-trope roots

---

[11] Charles, Jos. *feeld.* Minneapolis, Minnesota: Milkweed Editions, 2018. 15. Print.

here & here the girl

whose body i am, will be

girl unwelcomed

the ways home flooded under arctic water

& blueness is the familial body's honorific

in her unwelcomed throat, bells ring themselves blue

the ring ring in chest cavern   little

congenital agony means   helloo   helloo

unheard she is un-her she is ███

she tries to reach as heard or herd or her

in the blood relative lot of nothing,

but her version of trying looks like:

~~daughter~~ ~~(daughter)~~ *daughter* **daughter**

this appellation already devastated out of language.

this blood-appellation congealed

congeal: to frost together, to coagulate, to slow the life of blood, to
turn liquid into husk to take the warmth of living away, to still the
measure the record the document, to neutralize its information /
language, to opposite of resuscitate

to specter the present to ventriloquize the present. to be seen as a glimmer, a flicker, a glitter. to forecast the future-past.

"break. break, by all means."[12] the line. break. the line. break. the line break. break, break, the line break the family break. reappear the break from seen to seam.

Dictee, organized around the Muses, daughters of Power & Memory, art-work-quests for a mother tongue in the units of identity, creates a glossal language of tongues spoken directly to Life & Death, themselves.

❀ ❀ ❀

the exiled Palestinian poet asks, "what good is the poem?"[13] the state of good presents its insides, poems, its insights, poems. its tense

---

[12] Hak Kyung Cha, Theresa. *Dictee*. Berkeley: University of California Press, 2001. 79. Print.

[13] Darwish, Mahmoud. "Take Care of the Stags, Father." *If I Were Another: Poems*, Trans. Fady Joudah. New York, New York: Farrar, Straus and Giroux, 2009. 15. Print.

is a stomach, see, it currently carries the question of itself: where do poems go? pink in a volatile sea the poem determinedly to-be-determined. good is, too, a surround as border as boundary. the clouds counter-conquest the mountains. the air permeates the border. good breathes in. good breathes out. all will be good in time. from the view of the future: new time surrounds the ancient time. from the view of angels: what was our history surrounds your history. the state of exile might move from here to there as air into where we might be exhalatory:: right out of good's mouth we pray in the after of good, we pray in the inner of good. from the maw to the belly of the beast, the poem is the need to be free. what separation is the poem?

something made separate from itself . . . from "On the last evening on this Earth"

> we sever our days / from our trees
> . . .
> we contemplate mountains surrounding clouds
> . . .
> we are the night when midnight comes[14]
> . . .

severance of line break, severance of boundary, severance of language, how "mid" cleaves the night in two. these regimes so severely

---

[14] Darwish, Mahmoud. "Eleven Planets at the End of The Andalusian Scene." *If I Were Another: Poems*, Trans. Fady Joudah. New York, New York: Farrar, Straus and Giroux, 2009. 57. Print.

figurative they are literal again. what severances, the poem. what good is good for?

break. break visible the alienation. break, the verse. the line. break.

break this narrowed reality in which the "submission is complete" and "the expulsion is immediate" from land and posterity.[15] the imperialist monopoly on terror means we are always in captivity, always waiting for an allotment of annihilation.[16] here, i recall Sylvia Plath's "The Jailor," in which she imagines herself the negress:

> What would the light
> Do without eyes to knife, what would he
> Do, do, do without me.[17]

if resistance can only service repression, if revolution can only service regime, if clouds can only counter-conquest the mountains, we are locked in the unbreakable grip of always the same violences.

grown from my belief in the physic of a self: the field of my thinking my making. Newton's third law: *for every action, there is an equal and opposite reaction.* to be in a body equaled in opposition, our activity

---

15 Hak Kyung Cha, Theresa. *Dictee*. Berkeley: University of California Press, 2001. 79. Print.

16 ibid.

17 Plath, Sylvia. "The Jailor." *Ariel: The Restored Edition*. New York, New York: Harper-Collins Publishers, 2004. 24. Print.

and psychic material must serve some surplus some remainder some manner of remaining. form must give way, yes, the person-body & the state-body. the rooms the nests we tremble with our Black bodies, indigenous bodies, woman bodies, queer bodies, trans bodies, we can overwhelm with our collective activity.

❀ ❀ ❀

> What's the relation between the phonics of fugitivity, the phonics of maternity, and socialism? . . . This is about the place of fugitivity in a maternal song that is inseparable from transgressions of proper bourgeois kinship."[18]

i am devoted to excess not in service of containment. the feminine erotic well in me, as Audre Lorde speaks. it is my pleasure to exceed, catastrophically, these present strictures for the future, green.

The Angel Of Blank & poet of flowers, *terror blossom & wild (tender, too, however knobbed the notion)*, i am drawn to excess's ability to retrace, rearrange, & revise.[19] how might excess count backward past the point of zero, equilibrium, equal & opposing force? might there be some beyond-space of before-world, underworld, afterworld, over-world to which we might write?

[18] Moten, Fred. "Uplift and Criminality." *Stolen Life*. Durham, NC: Duke University Press, 2018. 132. Print.

[19] Leung, Muriel. "How To Find Each Other In the Dark." *Bone Confetti*. Las Cruces, NM: Noemi Press, 2016. 66. Print.

before there was any violence done to me, there was a seed. before there was a seed, there was the sea of my see, the ground to which i go, & the composition of stars from which i was born. & so, i am writing something of the palinode, which casts backward in time its retraction, forward in time the space of the unsaid, unmeant, undone. *forward.* it is forward which might exceed the apologist in palinode. back to & out of the seed of me i am less sweeping back debris & more obliterating the incitement of destruction, itself. good, the poem.

good, the gorgeous & grotesque catastrophe rearranging language, form itself, persistently. catastrophe, from the Greek, katastrophē, or sudden turn.

backwards-ing forward out of the Transatlantic catastrophe producing Black diasporic being, let us consider, too, Kamau Brathwaite's notion of the tidalectic. See the woman in front of her home on Jamaica's north coast, yardie sweeping sand from sand, ritual tidying, back, forth, tidal, as Brathwaite sees her: "tra/velling across that middle pass/age, constantly coming from wh/ere she had come from."[20] the twice trans tidalectic: to mother and land, Africa i am/b across water to recover the space before birth and the door of no return.

here, i recall a dear poet-friend's recovery of the grotesque in Cathy

---

[20] Brathwaite, Kamau. *conVERSations with Nathaniel Mackey*. We Press, 1999. 33. Print.

Park Hong's *Dance Dance Revolution* by way of Mikhail Bakhtin's *Rabelais and His World*, translated by Hélène Iswolsky, who writes "Degradation digs a bodily grave for a new birth; it has not only a destructive, negative aspect, but also a regenerating one . . . Grotesque realism knows no other lower level; it is the fruitful earth and the womb. It is always conceiving."[21] in *Dance Dance Revolution*, "Song that Breaks the World Record," the poem froths with the birth of its speaker and the birth of Korea's April Revolution:

> . . . (her heart a grave
> o infants, me tragic mum)[22]

the heart is a grave same as soil, is alive, makes new births. the heart is a grave exceeding grave, how language, here, exceeds the delineations of language, as Cathy Park Hong makes an "amalgam of some three hundred languages and dialects . . . [which] borrows from existing and extinct English dialects," including African American Vernacular English, Patois, Creole, Pidgin, Middle English, Latin, German & Spanglish.[23] a grotesquerie language always conceiving new language emerges matsutake mushroom-like, as described by Anna Lowenhaupt Tsing's *The Mushroom at the End of the World: On the Possibility of Life in Capitalist Ruins*. the matsutake's under

[21] Bakhtin, Mikhail. *Rabelais and His World*, Trans. Hélène Iswolsky. Bloomington: Indiana University Press, 1984. 21. Print.

[22] Park Hong, Cathy. *Dance Dance Revolution*. New York: W. W. Norton & Company, 2007. 41. Print.

[23] ibid. 19.

world nutrient networks nurture industrially ruined forests back to thrivance, defeating the notion of the individual, teaching us to coexist in "conditions of precarity . . . without the promise of stability."[24] to make a home in ever otherness, revolution, transness. & how to organize a future-body countermemory for the future? this simultaneity of birth & death work, mother womb & mother tomb, in *Dance Dance Revolution*: a multi-diasporic bodily grave, a fruitful earth, a field from which many revolutions might emerge into a Revolution the shape of Earth.

❀ ❀ ❀

might excess be the future enacted by way of past tense? the hearts which gushed so we will live. what retraction-might the redacted daughter writes.

a poem

curtsy, nod, alight into obedience along the branch the switch the beast. beauty sweeps back, & forth the beast breaks wood, glass, the skin which holds the heart, it leaves & bleeds. everything out of place: the lindens & the bees displaced by degrees. sweeping beauty retraces the everyday catastrophe of fists, retroacts a broom across fallen

---

24 Tsing, Anna Lowenhaupt. *The Mushroom at the End of the World: On the Possibility of Life in Capitalist Ruins*, Princeton, NJ: Princeton University Press, 2015. 2. Print.

skin shells & open sea sores, rearranges red dust to catch light at maritime, glitter by the lesion, aqua-maroon.

revision: bruises sound like sunsets.

revision: *she sets the sun on me, repeatedly.*

❀ ❀ ❀

its palinode:

bleak, blank, break into leaf along the branch the beast the you tree. a bud: a future green: a parting way. beauty embryonic shoots, beast is but a seed she leaves. the sky un-bleeds & she be leaves: heart-shaped leaves: the linden & the bees. seed, the forlorn fist forgotten by sky. beast, no beauty will cry for you. the night sky catches the light, glitter by the lesbian, obsidian-swoon.

revision: sunsets sound like sunsets.

revision: *what will she do, do, do without me?*

❀ ❀ ❀

separation: the poem: for good: for the future

it is not senseless, this violence of resisting & becoming. it is the violence of making, of one thing out of itself into another. see: the dictive tethering lineage & lineation.

in poetry, my mother tongue, twice trans nest which makes me possible, i seek to write, conceive. poetry is not a singular language, but the languages within language, marking the space of nothing as witnessed by way of feeling, an outside-inside. affect provides infallible testimony that i exist. out of sight. poetry. out of mind

in "The Inarticulate Affect," Claire Nouvet writes:

> The affect is mute . . . Muteness does not mean that the affect is simply voiceless. It is not the absence of voice but the condition of a voice condemned to remain unheard . . . "mute" comes from the root *mu* from which are derived "to murmur," "to moan," "mystery" as well as the Latin *muttum*, which gave the French *mot*, "word."[25]

dear reader,

i address my tone to you.

let us carry Robert Frost quoted as "a poem is the emotion of having

---

[25] Nouvet, Claire. "The Inarticulate Affect: Lyotard and Psychoanalytic Testimony." *Discourse* 25.1/2 (2003): 239. Print.

a thought while the reader waits a little anxiously for the success of dawn," as poetry is thinking with feelings. poetry is, perhaps, then, some murmuration in the touches of words we call a poem.[26]

placelessly, mending the work of others, perhaps some other i love.
to be able to see the stitch. how the chromosomes
of the fetus long-linger in the person who carries them.
then the breaking of family body & what fragments,
threads are left to see?[27]

filiform, filamentous

history pleats & in its fabric-fold, in the surviving
edge, the survivor, the space
to be a three-dimensional see

what *even* can a poem do?

in a lyric mathematic, can there be any quadratic
recovery of the subtracted overboard
& burned?

---

26 Belvis, Matthew. "Unknowing Lyric." *Poetry*, Mar. 2017. Web. Dec. 2018.

27 Girmay, Aracelis, panelist. Question-and-answer session. "Margin, Margin, Magic," 27 Apr. 1019, Goldwin Smith Hall, Cornell University, Ithaca, NY. This is adapted from the Q&A response via video conference.

if i graph love & loss, will i form a parabolic
arc from world to underworld
an ever-long lyric 'u'

to project forward the sum things, what can be different.

later, in "The Inarticulate Affect":

> the "poetic spirit" in action, "en acte": spirit acts by opening itself to "the indefiniteness and unfinishedness of linkages, indetermination." This disorder, this opening to and of indefinite linkages, is the very condition of "fecundity."[28]

how different our lives would be, dear reader, if never was the Freudian word "disorder" placed on me & where, in place, i was always named "fecundity."

❀ ❀ ❀

to life the life, to put life back in where there was only a rumor of life, a murmur of heart, to combust the nest, its architecture, "to not repeat history in oblivion."[29] i write against the blood garden's congealment

---

28 Nouvet, Claire. "The Inarticulate Affect: Lyotard and Psychoanalytic Testimony." *Discourse* 25.1/2 (2003): 241. Print.

29 Hak Kyung Cha, Theresa. *Dictee*. Berkeley: University of California Press, 2001.

to re-make the self, to remap sounds & make new sense, to newly associatively leap

from birth to revolution

poem press into the nothing nest

earth gasp, mother coo

be the blank. be the bleep.

reader, be where your bones loam.

fecund, fecund, fecund, fecund, fecund, fecund, fecund

unto the nowhere that holds the stars & everything else

all the monuments of here go bust along the way

rip in the sky   rip in the family-earth

Nebula Elsewhere

the poet of flowers

Bloom Psychotherapy

the nest of nothing

The Angel Of Blank

(puberty too)

Goddess

epi-visage from The Angel Of Blank

already devastated out of language. a martian & yet i March more mother than mutter. sad nutter she is. the poet of flowers. engorged by gorgeousity, where with all her sound goes lunar over the stars. each word a sister moon passing light into constellation with dark side. there is great darkness & grave darkness. to borrow & bling cannot forever. yes, a stellar nursery of earth is likely necessary. more place than person, the divine. she would make a garden of a single tree: e, pit, o' me. a denizen of gong. another gone she sheds she says *she leaves she leaves she leaves*. i am not the blank of blue. i am not the ambient above. what capital celestial combinate 'g'? i un-theorize gravity. i am elsewhere in the water (**drink**). come brackish combusting the enlightenment of a neuronic "no." *come poet. come infertile flower. grieve in the green intravene of us & we will leave this never-now this nothing more dust than dust* . . . earth, girl, she is everything's grave. reader, be where your bones loam. to this hole-hearted sunder, in Goddess, we must.

never-now nothing dust dust

suppliant women

silly heralds, foulers of words, won't you spake the wreath around my mother's grieving neck, her sea-spout sky holes, this whir of weeping ozone. heed her tempest season of *no*. my garden in the dead. ring around the newest eye. a tomb. aground. circumspect & shed: your hands. plead for holy spring & pierce your tongues with thorns. mercy is not my mother's name, nor is yours

stolid greens she will make of you:

whisperers naught -/- air to air.

building the barricade

what will survive? record or rock, the sound / the sand. after the
barricade blew everything the color of hammered midnight overhead,
you learn even fear ceases in the aquarelle of eyes-/-curl-in, light-leave.
belly-up bombs arc the poem of fire into saltwater. drink. lay the wound,
say the wound. the robin's-egg blue of an eye accounts the dead.

dead, doing, dying, live

the dust & light refraction
you leave behind quiver rain
into bow & lo the heir
an arrowed neck a narrow art
braced against wind doe
wet excess she shivers
an expectorating chorus spectral
the arc into air
small hark sky reigns
o'er years Goddess
blotting into view

death is made
of visible hues

dis · cover

rather than find first or
to make known
maybe, instead, meaning to skin
as in Prometheus the Skinner
foraging fire from the temples
of the gods   the soft tissue cost
dis covered
the infernal head holes
are known & first
remember light & uprise
holes in their heads

subjectivity

she is a me or she has a me or she is not
her body, though i do not know what she would do without it.

i have a self that exists inside every version of her.
there are years' worth of skin she did not recognize
an i or a self inside. i am attached to.

as a child, she labored under a mild obsession with kites.

every second, her cells labor under the in-
structions of DNA, hormones, the amount of sun
she does or does not become. in cell replication,
DNA is severed, copied, & stitched without
error. living is something like this, though the
tears are uneven & each seam shows.

if her body is infallible, then i am a sequence
of errors. i am commatic, incessantly throwing myself
onto her face always
turning away. luna, see, i am perfect as rarely
as the occurrence of syzygy. there is a third party
haunting every encounter with its planetary body.

my unrequited desire is a fool of gravity
& the helical structure of time. & effort. & i am looking into
the hole inside form that is trans-chronology & trans-failure
trying to fall in.

once, she was gifted a kite, but the wind ob-
structed the head's attempt to fly.

if hurt makes perfect, then i
blame the idea of god & her body which members

everything. i intervene in verse: the hormones.
she is still. her body remembers all
of its phases. i hurl the anti-face that i am,
but it falls, as star's stalwart grief
light into the concluding grief
of craters & all the wrong names for moon,
as some mostly blue earth keeps spinning.

though the blue-eyed will of god damns me,
there are blue moons & moments
we fall into three.
these are the fractions of day called divinity.
these are the trinity of Goddess i know.

i am her angel, blank & spooled
to a rosen poet moon. every day,
i pray to She to be superlative enough to blind
& hover in sky, a perfectly unseen
blackness where god's name was.

mars poetica

my dust-life, red & rovered toward. the poems are jurassic,
rewinders of life's alien center. a lake was here! eye sea
i see. all the years of your smallest material.
where water has gone. desert planet for rest

Nebula Elsewhere
the poet of flowers
Bloom Psychotherapy
the nest of nothing
The Angel Of Blank
(puberty too)
Goddess

redwood forest

yield the farthest reaches of trees
yield their feet & me leaned

into air we skim our bosk to breeze
into buds knuckle-green the way they live

for leaves to exceed the us we are
forest to jabber the air the air the pubic air

at twenty-six, hugs are dangerous

right breast, oh, how i have longed
for your rippling shape & these pangs
i sing in the ear of glee
how this hurt means the dream
me is cracking world shell true
&, oh, how i catalog my pain
in the book of pleasure to feed
the whisked yolk i am
to One Day & its red, red mouth

state wax, state wane

step by step i am terrified
bottled light inside the body
scan blinking nerves wonder
the feet & hands i splay i split
at pelvic wish full fold genital
lever pull making belief happen
stance array my limbs luciferously
look at me god's very manus
who pushes a button on looking
i do not know male or female
a fulcrum as genital as wrist
per this i will disco into humiliation
machine that i am flashing surveillance
daily the world whir alarms merely
as i appear

color is a transitionary state of emergency

at the level of flesh   yes epidermis subcutaneous
fine   look threads upon flesh   look vellus
uplifting touch   slight pricks above my
bust   look elephant leaves, pines
of evergreen, tower trees their thawing be
the smallest breeze, falling leaves
rock to sleep over garbage
bin green, feather faint impactor, i alight
without a sound into the gender
compactor, this landscape inverse
of laughter

i am a part in a park   the eyes
& sneers   to be observed queerly i
live sometimes in stares the uncloseted
feeling of peer & pier   there is
no banister brandishing the safety of being
entered   i have not the water
nor the weight to be ascended & descended
i just fall as does my name say swaying
to the rapture of breeze into the
leavening green to ground to queen
grass of which i seed beneath earth surface
unfleshed from a freakish flash trapped
in the space of see to unblinking
see.

earth-time is a place, a magnificence
of every leaf billowing in ecstatic
grief, how all my breath & subterraneous heart
a girl was, here—
from the view of dirt—everywhere
i am see'd

please in ultramarine

with a line after Jos Charles

street lights car
lights cut themselves across
the water's face just so
i am finally rayed

under elder stars
ambience is splayed
& centered how eyes cir
culate my circumstance
darkly i am under stand
grateful to be "no one"
breathing next-to-"sees"

is the face i could be
long to greet sea in homophone
ick surface i can't even peer
the substance i am i am laid down
a pier longing off into blue becoming

she harvests herself

black, perforated article of feminine
investment—how indentured the chest
to tight lines which draw the eye
to query beheld in the choke close
space of interrogative her bra screams
for her

think apples, cherries, melon seeds fleshed
in red think face peeled back & set
to teeth, surgery she is recalled to
ground to grow green in the face
there will be so much blood

terror is yeast to her daily bread
she shivers in sheets of flight
is risen & broken open into
fission pitted across her chest
light is juiced—an x is marked
in bra straps *dig me out of the future*
she wishes every day
to be melon'd

puberty 2

little commas of hair
how patient you have grown

in your near-vellus winging of air
breath as ineffable feathers

sentence long as skin
legs lift to the mouths of skirts

clause after legged clause punctuated with
wave crests frothing wide as birth

my girlhood, an unabbreviated breeze

self-sentence

to life my life o-seed that i am
to spit out the shell
blasted bits i gestate
myself inside myself like a comma
nested inside the sentence
my skin , cells, shells, spew

what is the grammar
of my flesh within my flesh?
vagination vagination
what is my face's appellation?
my brows bones jaws lines
break the jaws lines break
the skull shell spew

i am a finger like a comma
emerging like a margin
grown into an i with her head
attached at every chromosomal coordinate
in space ex-o-skeleton I leave
from seed to unwinding seed

queer "I" into an ampersand wing
& am everywhen whirling over myself
one foot planted in the past tense plane
wing fingering the future
to feed my lower lips
hand-to-mouth the will & pleasure

Certificate of Live Birth

you arrive on a friday, with hail & vast
moving gray above small window
of white light, as a wound
which might be a passing through
of particulate ultra violet waiting
to arrive in sight, our adjectival
see. will it be violent, our photographic
ring around the light?

we inviolate what we can't see,
revelate its arrival with our question:
boy or girl?

please, let the unseen speak in me.
there are stellar nurseries we cannot grimace.
i am a certificate of a bright somewhere.
you are a poem passing through
the membranes i have moved, mountainous you,
head up-of the interrogative blue

(a palinode)

CERTIFICATION OF VITAL RECORD

VIEW PRESENCE OF WATERMARK HOLD TO LIGHT TO VIEW

STATE OF MARYLAND
Department of Health and Mental Hygiene
Division of Vital Records

CERTIFICATE OF LIVE BIRTH

1. CHILD'S NAME (First, Middle, Last, Suffix)
   JASMINE REINA REID

2. TIME OF BIRTH (24hr)
   11:56 AM

3. SEX
   Female

4. BIRTHWEIGHT
   7 lbs 7 oz

5. DATE OF BIRTH (Mo/Day/Yr)
   April 11, 1992

6. COUNTY OF BIRTH
   Baltimore City

VITAL

PRESENCE OF WATER ARK HOLD TO LIGHT TO VIEW

STATE
ment of
vision o Vital Re d

A LIVE BIRTH

NAME
JASMINE

BIRTH

SEX
Female

B R IGHT

AT BIRTH
A 1, 2

COUNTY OF
more

of devotion, angel

layers deep in song my heart sounds
like a melodic siren thin as rope
the smallest girl jumping by the second
cover your ears with the sound of my body
slapped with pavement ambling
graceful as it can the reverse gospel
grooves jukes planes angles
my heart would angel
of devotion
can you hear the plea pumped in ecstatic gestures
of will like will to live like one day
i will be cut open rearranged
& put back together this is the sound of blood
having done its best now at the edge
of a cliff or a knife
waiting for the right
moment to fall in stereo
my heart gives & does not give
in or out or up squeezing by the second
a future i will live yes
in page & screen & too in form
yes a skeleton rivered in yes
yes yes my body is a future
ringing with yes is

Nebula Elsewhere
the poet of flowers
Bloom Psychotherapy
the nest of nothing
The Angel Of Blank
(puberty too)
Goddess

universe out there
universe in me
—(a) jasmine (in a vine of jasmines)

interlocutor litany

Goddess body   girl body
invisible body   swallowed burred body
backyard body   some body   sum body
say body   ex-spleen body
under stand body   pleas re-leaf body
ear-marked body   poor us body
sum day body   sew long body
body under state   body under space
constellate story body   first-person glory body
third-person horror'd body
"i" line body   eye-lined body   see body
seed body   breathe body   best body
bestiary body   infant times body
sky-made body   eaves of grass laid body
feathered body   unfettered body
unfeathered body   urn-nest body
sky (weight) body   sky (way) body
earth gift molt of body   body under body
body-undid-its-body   emerging body
birdling body   burst-sing body
sky-word: body   flew free ex-spelling itself body
grief-celebration body
body soars sees its pieces black on a page girl archive body
new feather-fangled body
new distance multi-valent body
new arrangement body
a new day spent in a body

girl is only everywhere

at the new students reception
the halls of my sisters all
girls school a fishiness in me
to be a flit inside blue jumpers & white
blouse a classroom myself so split
with nerves so yarn i am pearled
to my mother's side
tall-headed words shucking table
new girls all
oy polo blue i am skimmed this fall

where all, we flowers

where all with flowers your first bloody lips
in grass from garden backyard toy chest hours
the thing is wrath epitaph sepulchral thirst look
Chesapeake look lord Baltimore ma
her Sunday word slammed closed inside you
you the girl who doesn't get barrettes
no bowl of braids heads down the stairs ma is
a long well away night air flotsam winter
granny mama sees you she lingers in light
saint like above up lets your legs toddle alone
travel steps abaloneously you are slipping already
out of mother harbor baby blue your body
whorl struck by every knuckle ma ma ma
no daughter of pearl

trans: atlantic

& this is how: become
the family "freak"

heads heave
along the cross-

hung hall.
be a saltwater harbor

in a corner of carpet.
even blur that child-

hood stain of vomit
as you fore-give

your every self
& any else that pours your red

water back into the atlantic.
cry, but take

each of their lords in vein.
athena, athena out the brain . . .

Apocrypha: i exist in every world

at the checkout line. at the 7-Eleven.
under the scanner's rabbit eye. you
call me forth to swallow my core.
you ugly man. you language lecher.
your dumb tongue shucks me numb,
numb. numb inside a fluorescent stripe
is where the word river dies. the split of your mouth
& drown my dress the people'd streets
my body of running water. i hoped knot,
hoped not, knew wood, knew would,
be called, you called, my fall-faul-
not-my-fault. god, register-man, centripetal
slur, you *sir* my solar sister distant & stark. sinew
starts. Goddess is comma'd green. Goddess is holding water
spinning me up back to me. shithead man.
you are wrong. i will flee the sea-
way into the sky & gorge. fugitive

comet, impactor, i finger the night,
my chlorophyllic streak. in fact,
secreted dawn. sol i estrophylic gleam.
inter-suckle-honey-stellar
dyke of the universe.

perigee

rose this jackknife moonlight
up my deleterious papers
cratered as words crumble
soot in the bright
body free of its deteriorate
names horse black deaths
ink now see me
daughter'd where light
does & doesn't a parent touch

concatenate theory: a cosmology: a hole

shreds of grass & sky   second sea
morning-well   the future tense tunnel
i pulley waters   "i am"   "i will"

tomorrow i was cut on sight   a first breath back-where i will be
a hurt her harrumphing herd hymen hallelujah
a rose garland   i'm going to   have been
in the room where fault faults
g/lance   ob/gyn

oh me   oh my   again at the original wound
hemoglobin-cluster of hooves   branches blustered
at a mere river   returning tinsels of time
seconds irrupted into hours

ours   a broken "be"   all of me as lief   as tween
as love   my past-perfect-future-present person
look   the blood is falling   failing   ripples ripped
contractions   death to concentricity
everything dark   outside in
un-mitosis me

i did not become, but i was, i am, i will be, born

i was under water the first i heard my name
many'd as rain or the shower shooting its heads
starry ringing against my naked chest

jasmine, jasmine, jasmine went a-belling my breast
telling of buds to come, the nursery in me
as three black planets leaned, their orbits thrown

'aster, listen, my head a black planet
my nipples black—listen—round rings round a
jasmine trinity.: gravity song.: labor ring

dearly beloved

these strings excite my hands
across time
in different hands this time these
strings arrive
          what music.   swings
different hands mine & those
i held this song in mine
i swing & swing my dust
into the sky
pull on strings   push a stream
of legliness   higher higher
strings she sings *you are who i've*
waited for
she hands me my hands in strings
i hold i swing, swing up high
she hands me hands in swings
& swings she is bald & says
          don't go
&, so long, my stream of leaves
& leaves i so long fling
aside my fly & plead to beloved
all along
she plays for me a set
a half ring breath   & me
the rest   wing breath swing set

Traverse Town

with tongue, it starts. she
comes. home
is a meeting. where
times happen. together
we traverse. town
where loss is. materially
we are all found

she

black
                              how
                    lines
        query
space
      her

   ink
                           face
                     surge   is
gr   gr
                           so much blood

                                       daily
      sh   sheets
                   broken
                                      her chest
                                an *x* is
                          dig
she wishes every day
to be

stars poetica

the poems light up one another, syllables, leaves,
my body squiggles between, queer as a star system,
the blackest ink bridging everywhere's sky.
night, i am, earth become heart, warm in the dark.
the poems tell me where my body will be,
far & made of siblings, an interstellar poet tree

NOTES

"escape velocity"

"batty bwhy" is a play on a spelling of a Jamaican Patois word that is a homophobic/transphobic slur.

"Nebula Elsewhere"

"gyell" is a play on a spelling of the Jamaican Patois pronunciation of "girl."

This poem contains a reference to Kamau Brathwaite's *conVERSations with Nathaniel Mackey*, which reads

and she was tra
velling across that middle pass
age, constantly coming from wh
ere she had come from—in her
case Africa

I am also interested here in the chemical structure of water, the covalent bond.

"Goddess writes"

"Resuscitate" is used here in its (rare) noun form, pronounced ree-sus-suh-tuht.

"~~daughter~~ ~~(daughter)~~ *daughter* **daughter**"

Here, I use the word "overseeing" in the obsolete sense of "to see excessively," to which also is carried that overseer of the plantation.

"The Moon and the You Tree"

This poem is after Sylvia Plath's "The Moon and the Yew Tree." Yew trees are commonly found near graveyards and churchyards.

"a stroke / of dirt"

In geology, a horizon refers to a layer of earth. The layer of rock from which younger rocks are formed is called "parent rock."

"the nest of nothing"

This poetic essay was written in collaboration with many texts. See the footnotes therein.

"*suppliant women*"

The title of this poem references an ancient Greek play of the same name by Euripides. The poem takes up the voice of the mothers of the dead, with an appeal to Demeter, goddess of the harvest, the earth's fertility.

"*building the barricade*"

The title of this poem references a collection of the same name by Anna Świrszczyńska, trans. Piotr Florczyk, inspired by the poet's participation in the Polish resistance to the Nazi invasion and occupation.

"*please* in ultramarine"

The line "darkly i am under stand" follows Jos Charles' poem "LII." from *feeld*, in which she writes, "it is tragyck / bieng undre stood."

"puberty 2"

The title of this poem references Mitski's album of the same name.

"Apocrypha: i exist in every world"

The word "apocrypha" refers to the books that have been removed from the bible because they are believed to be of doubtful or spurious origin or authorship. Here, I take Apocrypha as Goddess of excess by way of disbelief for those who are outside of canonical human experience.

"*dearly beloved*" & "Traverse Town"

The titles of these poems are references to the video game *Kingdom Hearts*. The former is the name of the games main theme and the latter is the name of a world that exclusively houses people whose worlds have been destroyed.

ACKNOWLEDGMENTS

Versions of the poems held by this book have been published or are forthcoming in:

Academy of American Poets' *Poem-a-Day*: "Certificate of Live Birth" & "where all, we flowers"
Already Felt: "of devotion, angel"
Apogee: "chromosome death in a blood garden"
Indiana Review: "not a suicide note"; "at twenty-six, hugs are dangerous"; & "she harvests herself"
The Kenyon Review: "waterful jasmine"; "the nest of nothing"; & "concatenate theory: a cosmology: a hole"
The Poetry Review: "color is a transitionary state of emergency"
Southern Indiana Review: "a stroke / of dirt" & "interlocutor litany"
TriQuarterly: "Apocrypha: i exist in every world"
Virginia Quarterly Review: "a bed of beauty until alive, bury me" & "crush"
Voyages: Journal of Contemporary Humanism: "state wax, state wane" & "epi-visage from The Angel Of Blank"
Washington Square Review: "honey all over" (revised to "nectarean hymen")

Gratitude from the earth & star stuff that makes me possible to mentors: Aracelis Girmay, Lyrae Van Clief-Stefanon, Ishion Hutchinson, Valzhyna Mort, Fred Moten, Joseph O. Legaspi, & Joel Dias-Porter;

to poets: Chi Le, Anastasia McCray, Cristina Correa, Joël Díaz, Thiahera Nurse, Sokunthary Svay, Cindy Tran, Sébastien Bernard, Trace Howard DePass, Sarah Passino, Meagan Washington, Jasmine Jay, Catherine Chen, W.J. Lofton, Sa Whitley, Raymond Antrobus, Saleem Hue Penny, Chris Rose, Fanny Brewster, Gustavo Adolfo Aybar, D. Colin, Phillip B. Williams, & Muriel Leung;

to the space provided by Cave Canem, Poets House, & the Cornell University MFA Program to write many of the poems collected here;

to beloved friends-family: Jimena, river, Kimiko, Megz, Margaux, Angela, Steph, Natasha, Sonia, Alej, Devyn, Tara, Rhea, big sister Aya, Nico, & Rachel;

to my editor, Christine Stroud, & all the folks at Autumn House Press;

to my mom, with whom I am weekly healing the mother-daughter wound which has circumscribed much of my poetic life;

to my therapist, Anupama Kalyanam, the founder of Bloom Psychotherapy, after which a section of this collection is named;

to little jasmine, infant goddess;

& to my comrades & all named & unnamed who fight for dignity & liberation!

This book would not have been possible without your generous counsel, readerly shoulder-to-shoulder-ness, co-scientific study of poetry as a material force, commitment to craft as ethical-political all ways, nourishment, encouragement, love, faith in my vessel, & ability to see my cellular-deep worth as a person, flower, & poet.

These poems were written with indefatigable, invincible faith in the exploited & oppressed peoples of the world to become the revolutionary force we owe to ourselves & all life with which we are contiguous,

unto a world that meets the needs of all people & the planet~*

ABOUT CAAPP

The Center for African American Poetry and Poetics' (CAAPP) mission is to highlight, promote, and share the work of African American and African diasporic poets and to pollinate cross-disciplinary conversation and collaboration. Housed at the University of Pittsburgh, CAAPP's programming aims to present live poetry and conversation, contextualize the meaning of that work, and archive it for future generations.

The Center emerged in a 2015 brainstorming session between poets Dawn Lundy Martin, Terrance Hayes, and Yona Harvey, and was officially founded in 2016. Today, the Center is a space for innovative collaboration between writers and other artists, scholars, and social justice activists thinking through poetics as a unique and contemporary movement. In its effort to highlight, promote, archive, research, and generally advance the practices and epistemologies of African American and African diasporic poetry and poetics, CAAPP supports individual writers, artists, scholars, and others nationally and at a range of career stages and academic ranks. The Center also prioritizes providing opportunities for poets and artists outside of academia, in the Pittsburgh community and beyond.

ABOUT THE CAAPP BOOK PRIZE

Started in 2020, the CAAPP Book Prize is a publishing partnership between CAAPP and Autumn House Press with the goal of publishing and promoting a writer of African descent. The prize is awarded annually to a first or second book by a writer of African descent and is open to the full range of writers embodying African and African diasporic experiences. The book can be of any genre that is, or intersects with, poetry, including poetry, hybrid work, speculative prose, and/or translation.

PREVIOUS CAAPP BOOK PRIZE WINNERS

Terminal Maladies by Okwudili Nebeolisa

Winner of the 2023 CAAPP Book Prize, selected by Nicole Sealey

Discordant by Richard Hamilton

Winner of the 2022 CAAPP Book Prize, selected by Evie Shockley

Bittering the Wound by Jacqui Germain

Winner of the 2021 CAAPP Book Prize, selected by Douglas Kearney

The Animal Indoors by Carly Inghram

Winner of the 2020 CAAPP Book Prize, selected by Terrance Hayes

NEW AND FORTHCOMING FROM AUTUMN HOUSE PRESS

Bigger: Essays by Ren Cedar Fuller,

winner of the 2024 Nonfiction Prize, selected by Clifford Thompson

self-driving by Betsy Fagin,

winner of the 2024 Poetry Prize, selected by Kazim Ali

The Great Grown-Up Game of Make-Believe by Lauren D. Woods,

winner of the 2024 Fiction Prize, selected by Kristen Arnett

Self-Portrait as the "i" in Florida by P. Scott Cunningham,

winner of the 2025 Donald Justice Poetry Prize, selected by Major Jackson

Les Portes by Meredith Nnoka,

winner of the 2025 CAAPP Book Prize, selected by Cameron Awkward-Rich

Magdalena Is Brighter Than You Think by Grace Spulak,

winner of the 2025 Rising Writer Prize, selected by K-Ming Chang

For our full catalog please visit: http://www.autumnhouse.org